# The Bible Of Self Discovery

- Dealing with Low Self-esteem
- Self-love Guides For All Genders

Roger Peterman

## Table Of Contents

# Chapter 1

## Introduction To Self Discovery

This question appears to be extremely simple. Even while your name might be your answer, if you dig a bit deeper, things become more complicated. Can you identify your interests, personal care requirements, employment demands, and life objectives?
What a lot to think about! For some people, the answers are clear-cut. Others need to exert more effort.
You should think carefully before responding to this question. Self-awareness enables:
Make sure of your own physical and mental health.
Considering and being conscious of how you show yourself to others.
Examine self-acceptance and develop more empathy for yourself.
Locate your values.

Stop giving a damn what people think, and start driving yourself.
Within you lies a unique world. It is worthwhile to explore the hills and valleys. Like any great journey, going inside oneself may be frightening. It encourages you to confront the obstacles standing in your way, such as bad habits, fears, and other gremlins.
But what is self-discovery if not a noble pursuit? Here are some tips on how to get to know oneself better.
What are self-discovery and self-exploration?
Philosophers have been thinking about this subject for a long time. Fortunately, you don't have to shut yourself away to think. But you'll have to think about it.
The three pillars of self-awareness
These three essential steps make up the discovery process:

Self-awareness
Understanding your peculiarities also enables you to redefine who you are. You cannot alter your behaviour if you are not aware of it.
Discomfort
Self-discovery is a challenging process. It requires you to face parts of yourself that you might not find enjoyable. But how can you learn to love that feature of yourself or figure out how to mend it if you don't embrace it?
The process of self-discovery includes trying new things. While challenging yourself to try new things and stepping outside of your comfort zone can be scary, doing so will help you better understand your preferences.

Living Consciously
As you learn more about who you are, your life will have more purpose. More choices you make will reflect who you are and what you want to become.
Finding oneself through inner work
Inner work is the process of looking within to understand your true nature and experiences.

The practice of inner work does not entail dwelling on the past or fretting about the future. Rather, it is a regular habit of starting in your inner world to achieve a particular conclusion or objective, to live and exist in the world in a certain way. It requires examining our habits and behaviours that affect our well-being and making the required corrections.
You can help yourself on the road to self-discovery by setting aside time to actively engage in all three aspects.
observing and assessing your behaviour and personality
leaving your norm and comfort zone.
getting in touch with people to share experiences. Together, you can create a place where ideas may be exchanged and introspection can take place.
unorthodox call to action.

Why it's necessary to be self-aware

Peer discovery can be a helpful technique while you're young. They assisted you in forming your taste and acquiring effective interpersonal skills. You may also have learned about the perils of participating in unwholesome relationships or joining cliques.
Finding your identity as an adult may be difficult. Being confused by your surroundings or the people in them is easy. Do you merely like going to your friend's place when they have that band on? While having a close-knit group of friends is important, independence will allow you to carve out your path in life.

You will benefit from knowing who you are and what you can accomplish with your identity in the following ways:
Develop your demand-expressing skills.
Set clear boundaries.
Make better judgments in your career and personal life.
Limit your sacrifices based on values
love and acceptance of oneself
Take care of both yourself and your body.
risks of not understanding oneself
You are more likely to experience self-alienation or a discrepancy between who you are and how you live your life if you lack self-awareness. As a result, you could feel depressed, guilty, or ashamed over not realizing your full potential.

woman-in-discomfort-what-is-self-discovery
You face the risk of caving to the whims of other people. Your parents might encourage you to work in medicine, for example. If you're unsure of how you feel about drugs, it may be tough to avoid them, which could lead to issues in the future. It is not worth the risk to commit this magnitude to do what other people want you to do.
example of self-discovery

Everyone goes through some of the same things, even though everyone's route to self-discovery will be different. The following can be found along the path:
acknowledging your core beliefs and principles. Making decisions that are more in line with who you are will be easier for you if you are aware of what is important to you.
identifying your needs at work and home. Your daily life and job both benefit from certain environments.
You may save yourself from getting stuck in an inappropriate situation by being aware of what you need from your environment.
understanding your benefits and drawbacks. Being aware of your advantages will enable you to comprehend how to enhance the lives of others. You can get a sense of direction from this.
recognizing and understanding your mental operations. Numerous unconscious processes affect you.

every day. Once you become aware of your negative thought patterns, you can stop them.
increasing our curiosity Being aware of who you help you learn. You and others will ask better questions of one another, and you'll search for intriguing new information about the world.
being more accommodating to change Being aware of oneself aids in maintaining self-control throughout times of change. You'll improve your capacity for adaptation, much as a tree does in response to wind.
woman-asking-questions-what-is-self-discovery
What is the discovery process?

You may move forward with the advice we have for you now that you are aware of the importance of self-discovery and the numerous forms it can take. Let's first talk about what you ought to be on the lookout for.
Making observations while you explore yourself
There are many parts that makeup who you are. To learn some key aspects of who you are, please respond to the following questions about yourself:
What are your ethnic and religious backgrounds?
What inspires you? What wears you out?
Who do you hope to become?
What piques your interest?

What does your inner critic teach you about yourself? (Or aren't they?
What does a fulfilling life look like to you?

These are merely the start. You'll learn many things that are impossible to fully detail here because you are a unique person. You must pay attention and be open to these findings.
advice for beginning
Here are some suggestions for discovering your true self:
1. Get a journal going.
By jotting down your thoughts in a self-discovery notebook, you can better organize them. After a few days or weeks, go back to your writing and read it once more. Look for recurring patterns or new information. This is a great place to start your appreciation exercises as well. If you are appreciative, you'll be able to realize what's most important in your life.

2. Pay attention to the small print
Try to focus on the tiny nuances occurring all around you. You'll learn how to be more perceptive in other areas of your life, such at your job or in relationships with your family.
3. Think about yourself.
Examine your daily habits, attitudes, and deeds. Find out if they support you or the person you want to become.
4. Ponder
By meditating and practising mindfulness, you can unwind your mind. It's important to let rid of negative thoughts so that truths can emerge.

5. Self-confidence
The process of discovering oneself is challenging and delicate. Develop kindness and self-love. Have confidence that you can get through this.
6. Be curious without prejudice
Examine your stances, deeds, and core principles. Learn about their history and purpose for existing.
happy-man-with-trumpet-what-is-self-discovery
7. Exert yourself to the limit.
Try out some fresh hobbies and endeavours. take a class. Go on a trip. Through these experiences, your preferences will become apparent.
7. Exert yourself to the limit.
Try out some fresh hobbies and endeavours. take a class. Go on a trip. Through these experiences, your preferences will become apparent.

8. Learn from your mistakes
You can start unsuccessfully in a new career or area of expertise. Pay attention to these mistakes. They can educate you.
9. Making deliberate habit choices

Decide on actions that will help you develop more of the qualities you desire. Be patient since it takes time to form habits. Make a plan, stick to it religiously, and use a habit-tracking app.

10. Aim high

Your aims and goals can tell a lot about who you are. Don't be afraid to go after them; keep an eye out for them.

The next time someone asks, "What is self-discovery?" You will know. The process of discovering who you are is intriguing, even if you don't yet know it.

One of the most exciting things you can experience is knowing who you are and what you want to become. With the help of this method, you'll experience a renewed sense of purpose and get a little bit closer to who you are.

# Chapter 2

## Dealing With Low self-esteem

What precisely does low self-esteem mean?

Lack of confidence or the conviction that you are unworthy, insufficient, inept, unacceptable, or unlovable are examples of low self-esteem. Positivity and self-criticism might impact your behaviour choices, which could put you in a lonely cycle.
A person's mental health may be harmed by low self-esteem since it can cause stress, sadness, and eating disorders. Therefore, if you or someone you care about has this crippling condition, you must act immediately.
lack of confidence

Everybody occasionally criticizes themselves, but if you do it often or regularly have low self-esteem, you may have a problem. There are actions you can do to boost your self-esteem even though you might not be aware of what is doing it.
Self-confidence differs from self-esteem. The degree of confidence a person possesses is correlated with competence in a particular area of life. Even if one is quite confident in their abilities, poor self-esteem can still be a problem. Higher self-esteem does not always follow from increased self-confidence.

What are the telltale indications of low self-esteem?
Low self-esteem is manifested by:
expressing irritation and self-criticism
self-deprecating humour that emphasizes flaws while downplaying accomplishments
When things go wrong, don't look to others for help or place the blame on yourself.
You don't deserve to enjoy yourselves.
rejection of flattery
avoiding challenging circumstances because they might not end well
being too disturbed by compliments or criticism and feeling low, worried, ashamed, furious, or worthless

What triggers low self-esteem?
Early experiences may be a factor in low self-esteem. A person could develop unfavourable fundamental views about themselves if they struggled to measure up to their parent's expectations, experienced neglect or abuse, or felt out of place at school. These are deeply rooted notions that one holds of oneself.

Teenagers, particularly young females, may come across damaging notions and ideals on social media and in the media at large that lead them to believe that their value is defined by how they act or look. This could lead to low self-esteem and unfavourable self-worth perceptions. Both academic failure and bullying can lower one's self-esteem.
Stressful life occurrences like an unhappy relationship, a loss, or a significant illness can also contribute to low self-esteem.

What effects might having low self-esteem have?
If you have low self-esteem, you could struggle in relationships, at work or school, or with other things. When you are rejected or criticized, you could become quite angry and withdraw from social interactions and other pursuits. Any activity where you might be compared to or evaluated by others should be avoided.
Some people with low self-esteem may stop caring about their looks, while others may overcompensate by maintaining perfect hair all the time.

If you are the object of abuse or bullying, you may also battle with body image, engage in excessive drug or alcohol usage, and fail to speak up for yourself. Teenagers with low self-esteem may turn to drugs or alcohol to feel better or fit in, may have an unfavourable body image, and may begin engaging in sexual activity earlier than their peers.

Which illnesses are linked to low self-esteem?
Low self-esteem may be linked to a variety of health problems, including anxiety, eating disorders, social phobia, attention deficit disorder, and substance abuse.

How to become more confident
To increase your self-esteem, think about your areas of expertise and your strengths. Give yourself a high five for your accomplishments, no matter how small they may appear.
By putting things in perspective and exploring different options, you might challenge your gloomy assumptions.
Instead of worrying about things you cannot change, concentrate on the things you can.
Don't try to achieve perfection because that's unattainable.

Engage in activities you enjoy; it is simpler to be optimistic while you are doing so.
Give up berating yourself for making mistakes; we're all human.
be among people that encourage you.
Your self-confidence can increase by volunteering for causes.
Your mood can improve with exercise.
How to ask for help
If your low self-esteem persists, consult a medical professional, a therapist, a close friend, or a member of your family.

Self-Assessment Questions to Help You Feel More Confident

1. What behaviours and pursuits give you a sense of direction?
If you reflect on the times when you feel content and have a sense of purpose, you may feel more capable of bringing about positive change or advancing beneficial ideas. Realizing your mission may provide you with a sense of security or confidence because you will be aware of the substantial contribution you can make to a company or the people in your own life. Asking yourself this question can help you reconnect with the actions you may take to feel influential and fulfilled.

2. What are you good at?
One simple way to increase your self-esteem is to recognize your strengths. Knowing your strengths may help you value your skills and have faith in your unique abilities. If you have specialized training or qualifications, you may be pleased with your abilities and proud of the effort it took to earn them.

3. What does having a positive outlook entail for you?
Even if you might desire to feel more confident, it might be challenging to do so if you don't know what that word means to you. Consider how confidence might affect your life and how it might make you feel. This may help you to better understand why you want to increase your self-confidence as well as the steps you may take to do so.

4. What do you consider to be your fundamental principles and values?
Reconnecting with your core beliefs and ideals could give you more self-assurance. Finding causes or endeavours that are consistent with your basic principles might boost your confidence. If your actions and goals are in sync, you might feel good about yourself if your employer supports charitable causes or if you volunteer your time for deserving causes.

5. How can you make a challenging circumstance into a learning opportunity that will improve you?
Problem-solving could typically make you uncomfortable or cause you to doubt your abilities, but consider how you might feel if you use this experience to gain important knowledge. Your personal and professional development can be aided by your ability to conquer difficulty. You may believe that both pleasant and painful experiences can teach you anything.

6. How often do you doubt your own or other people's abilities?
Understanding your behavioural patterns can assist you in identifying problem areas and putting long-lasting change into place. If you notice that you constantly doubt yourself and your abilities, you could want to halt those thoughts and replace them with a positive statement about yourself or another person. By changing the

language you use to describe other people and yourself, you might feel more confident in your talents.

7. Who are the individuals in your life who improve it?
You might be able to list admirable traits in others if you are having problems naming qualities that you find admirable in yourself. Consider the influential individuals in your life and what they do to make you feel happy, grateful, or fulfilled. As you begin to appreciate the good in others, you'll notice that it becomes easier to see the good in both yourself and other people.

8. What can you do right now to feel good about yourself?
Take into account one thing you can do to advance toward your objective, whether it's improving your physical health or picking up new talent for the workplace. Making yourself proud can alter how you view your abilities and may inspire you to repeat this behaviour in the future. Working toward your objectives might help you gain bravery and self-assurance.

9. Do you know someone who possesses the self-assurance you desire?
By selecting a mentor or someone you respect, you can identify the kind of person you want to be and set achievable goals. Think about your friends or public figures who exhibit the confidence you aspire to have. Consider modelling their behaviour by paying attention to the routines and habits they establish to achieve their goals.

10. What are the three qualities you most want to possess?
By defining and achieving goals, you can appreciate your strengths and take pride in the talents that allow you to engage in novel activities. Consider the top three qualities you aim to possess and why they are significant to you. Making a plan to help you develop these qualities as you commit to making personal or professional success may help you feel more confident.

11. What three things most appeal to you about yourself?
Along with selecting who you want to become, think about who you are right now and what you value about yourself. Consider three qualities you value and how they might advance your career or improve your relationships with those in your personal life. Focusing on your character and personality traits as well as appealing aspects of your look, speech, or emotions is a possibility.

12. What routine might you use to boost your self-assurance?
One way to improve your sense of value is to create a daily routine that fosters your development. Consider one thing you can do every morning to make yourself feel great, and then observe how you feel the rest of the day to determine if it has an impact. While you might desire to do one big task to enhance your confidence, completing a small task every day might have a more significant long-term effect.

13. How did you overcome your fear?
Describe an occasion when you overcame a fear, such as when you went to a job interview that you weren't sure you'd receive or when you confided in your supervisor. Take into account how this process went, what you did to contribute to its success, or how you handled rejection. Whatever the outcome of the situation, knowing that you have the fortitude and ability to manage a trying circumstance may make you feel brave and self-assured.

14. What are you looking forward to?
If you have a major ceremony, an exciting holiday, or an inspirational ceremony coming up, think about focusing your attention on this upcoming event. Recognize your expectations and the factors that contribute to your happiness in this situation. For instance, you might be confident in your ability to address a huge crowd and inspire them with your words if you're giving a speech during a wedding ceremony.

19 Strategies for Combating Low Self Esteem
If you lack self-assurance, you might be interested in finding a way to change that. That it is feasible is fantastic news.
Low self-esteem is typically a taught behaviour, meaning that your current feelings of unworthiness were either created by focusing on your flaws or brought on by someone else. To get rid of this unwanted taught behaviour, you must begin forming new ideas and accepting the fact that no one is flawless. Here are some suggestions for getting over low self-worth and setting your life on the road to happiness.

1. Add some enhancements
Low self-esteem has several potential reasons. Some of these are beyond your control, while others are. For instance, if you have bodily dysmorphia, it could be detrimental to your self-esteem.
If you are overweight, for instance, you can start a mindful eating or walking regimen and start losing weight. When you exercise and eat healthily, your body will experience many positive changes that will have an impact on both how you feel and how you appear. a select few.

People can use this to take the first step toward improving their low self-esteem. Put the TV and computer away a few hours earlier and try to get at least 8 hours of good sleep each night if one of the things that lower your self-esteem is feeling fatigued all the time. To make it easier for you to unwind at night, create a sleep ritual. If you obtain adequate sleep, both your mind and body will remain healthy. Getting up early can also help you feel refreshed and energized, which will allow you to do more during the day.

2. Consult a mental health expert.
Anyone struggling with low self-esteem should seek help from a mental health expert. It might be challenging to boost low self-esteem because it frequently results

from trauma experienced as a child. Children who received excessive or little praise from their parents frequently struggle with low self-esteem. Such mental health issues should be handled by a professional. Thinking about how your parents felt about you or other circumstances, like the likelihood that they didn't congratulate you when you accomplished something you were pleased with, might exacerbate self-esteem problems. If you received a lot of criticism as a child, you can start to criticize yourself. a specialist in mental health.

3. List a few shortcomings.
I know it's easier said than done, but if you want to overcome low self-esteem, doing this is essential. You'll always be grateful for certain aspects of yourself. Try to understand that this holds everyone on the planet, no matter how perfect they may appear to be.
Putting more attention on your strengths than your flaws is one way to combat poor self-esteem.

4. Get rid of the inner critic
High self-esteem individuals are skilled at controlling their inner critic. Their minds are racing with happy ideas. Higher self-esteem does not result from positivity. Positivity is one of the symptoms of low self-esteem. You need to think of the opposite thought whenever those thoughts pop into your head. Even though it will first require some practice, you will gradually improve at naturally thinking positively. the difference between sadness, idle thought, and contentment. You're just asking this question to yourself because you feel insufficient. indicates you are insecure. Find out which specific thoughts are to blame for your low self-worth. Self-evaluation is important since only you can see what's going on within your head.

5. Employ a novel approach
People with low self-esteem frequently believe they are unable or underwhelming. They believe they lack the skills required for such occupations. Sadly, this is a prophecy that often comes true. You need to realize that you are stronger than you may believe if you want to overcome a lack of respect for yourself.
At first, try something strange, like enrolling in a photography or pottery class. You can even do dangerous activities like skydiving or parasailing.
Learn how to meditate if you've never done it.
Your degree of confidence will increase as you gain more knowledge or skills. When you start to believe in yourself, you'll realize that there isn't anything you can't accomplish.

6. Address issues with relationships
The demands of others can devastate your sense of self. Everyone errs occasionally. Unfortunately, occasionally they fail to admit their mistakes after saying anything inappropriate. Instead, you internalize it and take their assertion as gospel. It's crucial to understand that issues with relationships can arise in any conversation.

Be mindful of your words if you are furious with someone. Though you might not be aware of it, what you say can have permanent harm to people's mental health. Although you have no control over how other people will treat you, you do influence how they will affect your confidence. Try to understand how other people think. Try to find a solution that will make you both feel good if a conversation is going south. It serves no purpose to make others feel anxious or to make you feel uneasy around others. Praise frequently, acknowledging other people's accomplishments, and paying attention to people's sentiments before they develop into despair or worry are all fantastic ways to maintain positive connections.

7. Discuss your low self-worth.
This can benefit those with low self-esteem, even though it could appear a little weird. For instance, if your self-esteem is low, it can suggest that you be quiet in a meeting since you have nothing valuable to say. If this happens, "respond" to your low self-esteem by stating, "Yes, I have an idea, and I'm going to speak it out!" in a low voice, and then put that thought into action. Others may not agree with your idea, but that doesn't mean it wasn't valuable enough to share.
When attempting to improve low self-esteem, resist letting your negative feelings govern you. Act in a method that you feel is best for you to stand up against them and defeat them. And before you know it, your confidence will have increased and you'll be that much closer to accomplishing all of your goals.

8. Help others
Reinforcing one's feeling of self-worth via deeds of charity and morality is essential to building a strong foundation for it. If you're having trouble identifying your positive attributes, all you need to do is shine. You can get a lot of good feedback just by being helpful, congratulating them when they achieve, and overall being supportive. If you make someone else's life better, you'll gain from it in countless ways. Over time, your sense of worth will increase steadily. Realizing how much effort you're putting in will make you feel better about yourself.

At least once a day, try to show kindness, and don't be afraid to look online for opportunities to do so. You will ultimately discover that your mind is developing if you spend more time in the real world, which you are making for yourself to be a better experience.
methods for enhancing self-esteem

9. Attempt to relax.
One of the things that cause low self-esteem is ongoing stress. Therefore, it's important to learn how to relax. Negative thoughts will take over when you're under pressure and make you focus on your weaknesses rather than your strengths. This will make your anxiety and low self-esteem even worse.

Do something relaxing for a while. Ensure your well-being. Take a bath, play video games, practice guided meditation, sing or dance indoors, or do any number of other things. This will make you feel less anxious and more self-assured.

10. Be aware of the defensive tactics
An unconscious reaction to a situation triggers a defence mechanism. Protection can take many different forms, including suppression, denial, projection, and others. When you feel guilty, you may instinctively use defence mechanisms to prevent yourself from internalizing your bad actions, thoughts, or experiences. People with low self-esteem usually employ defence mechanisms.
without realizing it. Your self-esteem may have been harmed by having too many traumatic experiences, and you may have become defensive in the face of future painful events. We all use protection mechanisms, though, at some point or another. Be mindful to spot them when you find yourself doing them to prevent issues in the future.

11. Remain present-focused
Two other strategies for overcoming low self-esteem include learning to live in the present and letting go of the hurts of the past and worries about the future. To do this, engage all five of your senses: stop and listen for wonderful bird sounds, feel the breeze on your skin, breathe in the fresh air, and appreciate the sky's beautiful colour. All of these will help you stay in the moment and help you have the right frame of mind when making daily decisions.

12. Refrain from overanalyzing mistakes.
Your thoughts could hurt your self-esteem. You need to take care of your needs. Instead of obsessing oversend yoga ralattare emptsstempt to stop unpleasant thoughts at the source. Being conscious of your brain's activity is the key to achieving this. Every time a negative idea arises, simply say "stop." It helps a lot if you can believe it since it suggests that you are living in the present rather than dwelling on the past or worrying about the future. It gives you back your sense of authority. Those who battle with low self-esteem might then go one step further and replace their negative thoughts with positive ones.
Remember that negative ideas are just beliefs, not facts. Since you will make mistakes throughout your life, all you need to do is learn from them. There's no need to feel guilty or inadequate every time you make a mistake. Avoid letting ar stop you from learning.

13. Look after yourself.
Why would you be kind to others yet harsh on yourself? Treating oneself with the same respect, tolerance, and forgiveness that you would extend to your best friend is one way to boost low self-esteem.
Loving-kindness meditation is one way to sit and spend some time practising some love and kindness to oneself.

We occasionally fail to be as generous with ourselves as we are with our friends and family. When you accept and love yourself, you'll notice a surge in your self-esteem.

14. Be kind to yourself and acknowledge your strong points.
Self-appreciation and self-acceptance are two different but connected ideas. You cannot value yourself if you do not accept yourself.
Examine your life, recognize your strengths, and work on enhancing those areas. We all too often put all of our time and effort into something we know we can't do. Instead, decide on your area of expertise and speciality, and then focus all of your energy and perseverance there. We all have weaknesses, so stop being so hard on yourself when you perform poorly.

15. Develop new skills
It's time to kick bad habits and pick up new skills if your self-perceptions are true and you worry that your lack of confidence stems from your perception that you're not good enough. Starting to act positively is the key to treating low self-esteem. The most common phrase you'll hear is: "You're perfect just the way you are." And to a certain extent, that is true. But isn't life better if you're continually improving? Nothing is wrong with making an effort to get better. You can read books about communication if you and someone else are arguing verbally. If others have a bad opinion of you, try to be more considerate of them. You can find articles about how to dress when people make fun of your appearance.

16. Stop comparing your circumstances to those of others.
You do not have to live up to the expectations that society has for you. If you want to overcome low self-esteem, start learning to live your life and stop trying to please other people. Never compare your successes to those of others. Instead, set boundaries and goals and go after your dreams. Remember that each of us is special and has something to contribute. Once you learn to stop comparing yourself to other people, you'll find that you're much happier with yourself.

17. Abandon presumptions.
For the sake of your health, stop doubting yourself. It's wrong to subject yourself to this. If you feel uncomfortable with toxic people because you display signs of poor self-esteem, you shouldn't just take the abuse. Get rid of those people, not the other way around. Making a will help you feel more confident. The solution to these issues depends on whether or not you listen to yourself.

18. Do not criticize yourself
While you attempt to overcome your low self-esteem, remember that we are all only human. Everybody will err from time to time in their life. In reality, some people make a lot more money than others.
One way to raise poor self-esteem is to learn not to berate yourself for your mistakes. Instead, learn from that mistake. Keep it in mind and put it to use to make

sure you don't make the same mistake in the future. Always keep in mind that experience is the only way that anyone learns.

19. Spend time with upbeat individuals.
How we view ourselves has a significant influence on how we feel about ourselves. These things infrequently might have a lasting effect. Unbelievably, the individuals you were with or had interactions with in the past influenced who you are today.
If you want to feel good about yourself, why surround yourself with hateful people? Why hang out with someone who hates themselves or doesn't have any goals or aims in life?
Spend time with inspiring people. Attend conferences with people who will push you to accomplish the impossible and who genuinely care about your success.

Get to work on your sense of self.
Getting over low self-esteem takes a lot o ace. It seems to reason that there may be instances when you feel as though nothing is happening or that you are wasting your time. There will also be moments when you feel like giving up and hanging out with the same people because you don't have any other plans for your future. Don't let these conditions cause you to lose focus. If you persevere through your setbacks and keep going, you'll eventually reach your objectives and live a happy, fulfilling life.

# Chapter 3

## Temperament

Many believe that the people in our life can affect how our personalities grow, which can affect our decision-making about our careers and daily activities. Every incident, no matter how big or tiny, has the power to alter how we think, feel, and act. Our perception of ourselves may also alter when we interact with new individuals and bid farewell to friends and loved ones throughout time. This chapter will discuss the choleric, melancholic, sanguine, and phlegmatic moods.

Does Understanding Your Temperament Help You Build Better Relationships With Others?
A person's temperament defines how they act and present themselves based on personality traits and formative events. Your constant temperament determines how you react to situations. It is a method for locating enduring personality traits. According to one study, brain-stem functions influence disposition. Each person's distinct brain stem remains fixed throughout life. Contrary to popular belief, people can change even while the brain stem does not. A young child's personality changes with time.

People can add new behaviours to their temperament as they gain more knowledge of the world and develop them. Think about how children respond to stimuli and how their responses change over time. For example, a young child who turned to look at their mother's face when she called their name as an infant might turn and leave the room as they get older.
Whatever your personality, you should always strive to become a better version of yourself while still being proud of who you are. Since it's a miracle you're still alive, live life to the fullest.

Can you change who you are?
While your basic temperament is unchangeable, you may alter your behaviour as you get older and keep adding to your experience by changing the way you perceive the world. You can alter your perspective by being aware of how your surroundings affect how you think and feel. By understanding the four temperament types, you can change your behaviour if you've ever thought that you acted unfairly.
Four main temperament categories are recognized by psychologists when determining temperament. The sorts' names were once terms for humour in earlier eras. Humour in this context does not refer to what you think is amusing! Each characteristic of this archaic notion of medical knowledge is based on a Latin word.

People in the period held the belief that a person's temperament was established by the relative proportions of several qualities, which also had an impact on conduct. Galen of Pergamon developed this idea, which is a phenomenon known non as Galen's Prophecy and which defines many of the ancient terms you'll read about later.

These are the previously mentioned humour, and humorism is the study of bodily fluids that are thought to exist. People believed that a dominant presence of one fluid, which varies from person to person because everyone has varying amounts of fluids, defined a person's temperament even though in modern medicine, the names of the four temperament types have persisted.

Both the primary and secondary temperament types are likely to exist in one person. A person's personality and disposition can be made up of any mix of temperament types. Keep in mind that the descriptions that follow are neither diagnostic nor exhaustive; rather, they provide a summary of typical characteristics that persons with these temperaments may display. A lot of people will be able to relate to a combination of their descriptors with sanguine temperament outgoing and extrovertedwhwhoey are people-oriented. Additionally, they emphasize how individuals cooperate, attempt to be pleasant to one another, and are generally helpful. It is the most prevalent temperament type and often comes in primary or secondary forms.

Both men and women are equally likely to have this temperament type. Some persons are said to as "super sanguine" because they are so excessively chatty and active that being around them can be exhausting.

Characteristics of the Sanguine

A wide range of emotions and behaviours define the sanguine temperament type. They are the most adaptive temperament of all. Depending on their secondary temperament, they are capable of participating in practically any human activity. However, they do enjoy chances to interact with or change their environment.

Sanguine Actions

When you first meet someone with a sanguine temperament, they could make you feel like you've known them for a very long time. They are simple to talk to and get to know. They are extremely amiable, talkative, and gregarious due to their sociable attitude. They frequently lose track of time when conversing. However, if they get bored, children might quickly lose interest. How attentive they are directly related to how much they are enjoying the conversation or what they are doing.

People with sanguine temperaments are very energized. If they are thinking or feeling it, they will say up. They have no filters. Their overwhelming activity frequently leads to confusion and forgetfulness. This temperament type is characterized by intense competition. They oversee business, politics, and athletics. They also worry about performing poorly and receiving negative feedback. Most people want to be accepted and have the chance to succeed.

Phlegmatic
Phlegmatic temperaments, while also common, have a disposition that is almost exactly the reverse of that of sanguine temperaments. Although introverted and service-oriented, this temperament type will work with others to achieve a common goal. These people may come out as lethargic and lacking in overall desire or a specific motivation to attain a goal. The possibility of having a primary sanguine type and a secondary phlegmatic type, or the opposite, is also plausible.

The characteristics of phlegm
Since it is passive, the phlegmatic temperament type displays a special mix of characteristics. They are dispassionate, calm, and laid back. They can be indifferent and nice and are often happy to let others make decisions for them.
Phlegmatic temperaments tend to be more gregarious yet take longer to warm up to others. They are one of the temperament types that are easiest to get along with since they are so accommodating and tolerant. But they are resistant to change and stubbornly adhere to their rituals.

Phlegmatic actions
Calm, family- and home-focused lifestyles are traits of phlegmatic temperaments. They don't engage in social or environmental interactions. They also have a temperament that makes them incredibly devoted to their friends, and they will uphold a friendship no matter what the other person does or says. They are unlikely to make an effort to mend a broken relationship.

Melancholy
When most people hear the word, they immediately think of depression. Instead of being constantly unhappy, the melancholy temperament type or disposition is cautious. Melancholic temperaments are fastidious, quality-conscious, and intent on doing things well. In addition, if people observe them paying special attention to every last detail, they could be perceived as perfectionists. This is just another example of a typical temperament.

Melancholy Characteristics
The depressed disposition submits to authority. In unfamiliar situations, they might show signs of behavioural restraint and be cautious and uneasy, yet they might also lash out violently. They exhibit extreme reserve. This personality is factual, analytical, and sensible. To operate without worry, these people must have a defined action plan and strictly follow it.

Melancholy actions
Anxiety symptoms can be seen in adults with melancholy temperaments, and these symptoms may have been present from childhood. Possible worries include the future and what other people will think. They might also be concerned about possible

alternative historical solutions. As a result, they could come off as unwilling to live in the moment.
Even if they become disorganized, people with this disposition are typically well-organized. These people regularly arrive on time for appointments and anticipate others doing the same. To ensure they are making the best choice, they will acquire as much information as they can and ask targeted questions.
A melancholy disposition also makes a person suspicious and meticulous. They wait until they are certain of someone's intentions before they trust them. They have high standards for their relationships and find it challenging to establish them.

Choleric
The choleric temperament is the least prevalent of the four primary temperament types. People with choleric temperaments tend to set goals and see them through to completion. They exhibit favourable acts or dispositions as a result, and they advance constantly. They tackle everything with an effort to overcome all challenges and achieve their objectives. While this combination is less common than some others, choleric is more usually a secondary temperament.

Chimeric Characteristics
People with choleric temperaments are extroverted and self-assured. They are independent and strong-willed, and they don't show any signs of being low on energy. They frequently have quick minds and are mindssdsdsssnergetic and practical in their hobbies, yet they can also occasionally be sensation seekers. Their communication is direct and aggressive, usually short and even disrespectful.
This temperament type enjoys taking risks and becomes bored easily. They occasionally display aggression and strong opinions. They naturally make decisions for both themselves and other people. They could be rather domineering in relationships. Additionally, choleric temperament types often get less sleep than other temperament types.

Choleric Traits
The choleric temperament is characterized by creativity and extroverted behaviour. They never seem to run out of concepts or strategies, and they all tend to be doable. But they are firm in their beliefs and will not yield to peer pressure.
They may be sympathetic and support social issues, but they take their time forming close bonds in their personal lives. Even though they are not hesitant to meet and converse with new people, they probably only have a small number of close pals. They don't frequently exhibit empathy for others. They can be more easily misunderstood as angry because of their commanding demeanour and direct speaking style, but they are also quite slow to become angry. It has been a member since

Choleric Actions

Creativity and extraversion are traits of the choleric temperament. They never seem to run out of ideas or tactics, and they are typically all attainable. However, they are adamant about their convictions and will not cave ippppressurehey may be understanding and supportive of societal causes, but they take their time developing strong relationships in their private lives. Although they don't hesitate to talk to and meet new people, they generally only have a few close friends. They rarely show empathy for other people. They have a dominating presence and a direct speaking style that makes them more likely to be misconstrued as angry, but they also take a while to get upset.

# Chapter 4

## Love Language

To have a successful relationship, a couple must first learn about one other's love languages during the wooing phase. Sexual topics shouldn't come up right away in a relationship, but understanding your own and your partner's love languages is essential.

What does a love language exactly mean?
Do you have a buddy who, even though you would prefer a little romance, would prefer a spotless kitchen to flowers? That very phrase serves as a straightforward example of several love languages.
We all have various ways of giving and receiving love, and those differences may be the reason why occasionally emotions and sincere intentions are mlsInterpreted.
For instance, you might spend weeks finding the most amazing gift for a lover only to hear them say on their birthday, "I would've been satisfied simply ordering in and then cuddling up on the sofa together."
It's not always true that they don't appreciate you or that you erred. Simply said, they show their affection differently or disengaged gede stronger connection, more thoughtful partnerships, and less aggressive birthday and Valentine's Day festivities may emerge from knowing how you and your spouse prefer to receive and offer love.

What other types of love languages exist?
We need to be aware of the five different love languages and know which one best fits us.
Five primary types of love exist:
*Words of affirmation
*Quality time
*Physical touch
*Acts of service
* Receiving presents

The use of love languages is not just for romantic relationships. Additionally, they can be useful in your platonic interactions. We'll elaborate on it later. connecting love language with However, if you believe that this individual might be a partner

Words of affirmation
Verbal expressions of love, appreciation, and inspiration
You thrive when others encourage you, and you like constantly hearing "I love you." Increase your use of the phrases "I love you," "thank you," "you matter to me," and comparable ones.

Quality time
spending time and giving someone else your whole attention. Even Wash they see others, they feel distanced from each other when they don't spend enough time together. Have date nights, turn off your phones when you're together, and have a conversation over dinner about your days.

Physical contact
a connection created by sufficient physical contact.
If you're a "touchy-feely" type of person, being hugged or touched makes you feel the most loved. Hold hands and provide other signs of affection, and if sex is important to the relationship, prioritize it.

Acts of service
Selfless and caring actions make someone's life easier. You are appreciative when someone offers help without being asked for it; for you, actions speak louder than words. Making their food, taking care of a few errands, and ing gifts
is a concrete ways to show someone you care about them. You take great delight in providing presents that have been carefully chosen, and you place a premium on meaningful gifts. Bring your favourite treat home, design or buy them a one-of-a-kind gift, or surprise them with gifts different than those given on particular occasions.

Words of affirmation as a love language
Words of affirmation are the first love language, and they are used to convey love and gratitude, whether orally, in writing, in texts, or any combination of the three.
If you thrive on: this might be one of your love languages.
hearing "I love you," hearing compliments, and frequently hearing words of support
The secret to using words of affirmation is to be genuine and use them frequently. Send a text or a letter if you have problems expressing yourself verbally. What important is that you express your appreciation to them in words.
For a relationship, this can entail expressing your love for them more frequently or calling them periodically during the day to let them know you are thinking of them. Words of affirmation for a buddy might take the form of a text message saying, "You'll be fantastic!" before a job interview or an on their attire.

Here are some phrases you might use to express encouragement in platonic or romantic relationships:
I cherish you,
"I value our friendship greatly."
You've got this.
I'm so proud of you.
Thank you for loving me, supporting me in all you do, being my buddy, etc.

Quality time as a sign of affection

The second love language is quality time, which is exactly what you might expect: enjoying spending quality time together.

When individuals they care about make time for each other and offer each other their whole attention, a person whose love language is quality time may feel most loved and cherished.

If any of the following apply to you: You feel distant from a partner when you don't spend enough time with them.

Your libido is impacted by not spending enough time with your spouse or partners.

You put a lot of effort into scheduling social time.

Everyone has a different idea of what quality time is. Some people value having some time set aside to unwind with one another at the end of the day. Others define quality time as making time for shared activities.

When spending quality time, it's important to be fully present and free from outside distractions.

Here are some instances of how to show your love by spending quality time:

Before getting out of bed every morning, spending some time cuddling.

consciously planning a dating night once a week.

No matter how busy you both are, make time to get out with your best friend.

putting your phone away when you're talking or engaging in a shared activity.

establishing a ritual, such as taking a walk after supper or gathering for lunch once a week.

Physical touch

The third love language is touching. To be clear, this is appropriate, consenting physical contact, which manifests differently depending on the circumstance and the nature of your connection with the other person.

Physical touch is vital for those whose preferred method of expressing and receiving love is touch. They communicate and feel connected to others through touch.

If any of the following apply to you: You feel lonely or distant from your lover when you don't receive physical affection; (s).

When a spouse gives you an unplanned kiss or cuddles you, it makes you feel especially cherished.

You adore PDA and consider yourself to be "touchy-feely."

Your relationship with them will ultimately determine how you should and can interact with them. Physical touch can be used to convey affection through simple actions like hugging or cuddling. It may also involve additional sexual activity, such as kissing if it is acceptable.

Here are some instances of how physical touch can be used to show love:

kissing a companion goodbye and hello.

being open to receiving love, even in front of others.

lingering in bed with a partner before and after sleep.
scheduling sex, even if you have to prioritize it.
You can reassure them by touching them, holding them, or putting your hand on theirs.
Again, permission is required. Use these examples and don't touch anyone unless they've made it clear they're welcomed and welcome.

Acts of service.
The fourth love language is acts of service, and if you truly feel that deeds always speak louder than words, this love language will speak to you.
By actions, I mean providing the other with thoughtful, selfless acts. Keep in mind that these don't have to be romantic; they can also strengthen bonds with friends and family.
These are some indications that your love language may be acts of service:
When a spouse assists you with a task without having to be asked, you are over the moon.
You are the friend a friend needs when they are having a rough day.
You are constantly willing to step up and take action on behalf of the people you care about.
Giving someone a cup of coffee in the morning or running an errand for a busy friend or loved one are examples of acts of service rather than extravagant gestures.

Here are some examples of how you can show others love by performing acts of service:
without being requested or for a special occasion, taking them out to supper.
Making a bubble bath for a lover without any sexual expectations.
offering to watch the children for a friend so they may take a well-earned vacation.
letting them pick the movie they want to see, even if it's "horror," which you despise.
Buying them preferred flowers, soap, wine, chocolate, or whatever else they like just because.
Gift-giving as a love language
The fifth and final love language is receiving gifts. It must be made clear that this love language is not just for the materialistic or alleged "money diggers."

It goes far beyond just wanting material things for someone whose love language is gifting. For this person, the significance of the present and the thinking that went into it are both equally important. No pricey automobiles or diamonds are necessary.

Receiving gifts
You take the time to select the most considerate gift while presenting presents.
No matter how little a partner provides for you, you value it all.
When someone you care about fails to honour a special occasion with a kind memento, it hurts.

Giving gifts to express affection is not about being extravagant. Even a tiny present will be appreciated because it serves as a physical reminder that the recipient was given thought and care.
Giving gifts is someone's love language, so here are some ways to express your affection for them:
picking up their preferred treat on the way home.
Surprise them with flowers, whether they are picked up from the side of the road or purchased from a store.
sending them a sympathetic card for no particular reason.
bringing a memento of your first friendship, such as a photo from your first road trip, to your best friend.
selecting presents unique to your relationship.

How can I figure out what my love language is?
Remember how you show affection to the people you like, whether or not they are friends, relatives, or in romantic relationships, to figure out what your love language is. Do you enjoy bathing them in compliment? Or perhaps you decide to show them a lot of love by unexpectedly showing up to drive them from the airport? The most important approach to show someone you care may be to pick up the bill at breakfast or to pick something up for them while you're shopping when you see something you think they'll like.

Your love language is typically easy to identify by the way you show others that you care about them and by the way you want them to love you. Everyone can also relate to most of those languages, but every older person has one that speaks them you youuhem youtube several love languagesanaaandddor you might have one primary love language and a few secondary ones.

Differences between receiving and giving love.
You could have one love language for receiving and maintaining affection and another love language for giving love. For instance, you might want others to feel valued by your words of affirmation, but serving others is probably the major method you show that you care about them.
The receiving language—how you want to keep love and how those around you need to receive love—is another crucial thing to pay attention to. Given that the goal is frequently to make the recipient feel appreciated in the way that they like, the donor must be aware of the recipient's preferred love language.

how to determine your partner's preferred communication style.
Asking your partner which of the five love languages they most enjoy hearing is the best way to determine their preferred method of communication. This is the sole way you should express affection to them daily because it is their preferred love language. If you want to help them comprehend while they are trying to express their

love for you, you can also ask them which of the five languages they most usually use to express it to others.

Finding out what your major love language is and using it frequently might help you and your spouse better understand one another needs and support one other's development.

the bottom line

Knowing your love language is essential if you want your romantic partners and other significant others to know how to provide you with the affirmation you need. Knowing your partner's love language is also crucial since it should influence how you communicate with them.

# Chapter 5

## Ten Things You Should Never Forego To Be In A Relationship

1. Your self-worth, self-assurance, and belief in yourself
Depending on the relationship, we may either bring out the best in ourselves or feel uneasy and unworthy. If you discover that you have more self-doubt than you did at the beginning of the relationship, it may be time to investigate why your confidence has diminished. You should have a solid foundation in a healthy relationship so that you can travel the world and achieve your objectives. If your relationship makes you feel "small" and impairs your skills, that should be taken as a warning sign.

2. Your individuality and financial stability
Being in a relationship may be a great, loving experience. Always maintaining your independence and avoiding melting into one group identity is essential. Spend time with your friends, keep a separate bank account for yourself, and take up hobbies that don't always include your partner. Being independent is a healthy trait that consistently conveys the idea that you are in the relationship deliberately and not out of necessity.

3. Your Independence and Right to Decide
Never give up your principles or your freedom of choice to someone else. Compromising is essential, even though finding a win-win solution is desirable. Be aware of spouses who want to control you too much. Whether it is criticism of how you dress, cook and/or clean the house, or the friends you have, make your own decisions and refuse to be swayed into doing things you don't agree with to keep the peace.
You Are Entitled to Be You protect the "essential you" by never compromising on your primary attributes or identity. We all adjust to some degree in relationships, but it's important to avoid losing oneself in the process by trying too hard. Those you love will cherish the real you, with all your flaws. If you repeatedly strive to change who you are, your self-confidence and self-esteem will suffer. It may also be discouraging.

5. Your Contentment
We occasionally find that our dread of being alone outweighed our desire for genuine happiness. As a result, we keep being in relationships that do not bring out the best in us. By maintaining healthy relationships out of apprehension about the future, we cause a great deal of harm to ourselves. As you only have one relationship, try not to waste it away in an unhappy one. Give up a relationship that over time makes you

feel less fulfilled and happy. Think about the reasons behind your dissatisfaction and whether your current relationship has anything to do with it if you feel undervalued.

6. Your Goals and Dreams

Never compromise your objectives to keep a relationship. A partnership should be a platform from which you can pursue your goals rather than something that keeps you trapped and unhappy. Jealous and/or insecure partners who want to keep their gifted

mate close to where they think they have control and try to repress a creative, passionate intellect. If this describes your relationship, you need to accept that it is unhealthy. Healthy partnerships encourage exploration and help the individuals involved progress rather than stagnate.

7. Current Relationships That Matter To You

Never give up your incredible and loyal friends for a love commitment if you have any—which can be hard to discover. Any partner that expects you to give up your relationships with friends for them is selfish and potentially possessive. A healthy relationship can coexist happily with family and friends. Consider it a red flag if your partner makes an effort to put space between you and your friends and family.

8. Have self-respect

We occasionally transcend boundaries that we wouldn't normally consider doing for the sake of love. If you allow yourself to be treated disrespectfully or engage in behaviours that you feel are humiliating, this is still another sign that the relationship is unhealthy for you. Never cede your entitlement to treatment that is respectful and decent. If someone crosses this boundary, you should fire them right away. If you continue with this course of treatment, it will worsen, and you will despise yourself for allowing it to happen.

9. Avoid becoming your partner too much and losing who you are in the process.

When we devote ourselves totally to a relationship, we frequently take on our partners' interests and habits. This procedure is perfectly OK because "mirroring" builds our bonds and brings us closer together. The problem occurs when we don't

have a strong sense of who we are, to begin wi,  and e eating our own identity, we absorb features from our partner. We risk losing our ability to make decisions for ourselves and deviating from the path of true self-discovery if we allow our relationships to dominate us too much.

10. Your Decision-Making Capability

Think of your decision-making skills like a muscle that will weaken if it isn't utilized frequently. We are less likely to think independently in the future the less we rely on our partners for advice when making judgments. This doesn't mean you have to make every decision yourself; rather, you should be aware of any tendency you may have to talk to your partner before making a decision, especially if it's relatively insignificant, like a little purchase for the house. Take charge of your own decisions, no matter how small, and keep doing so. You can maintain your sense of independence and your potential for self-sufficiency by doing this.

# Chapter 6

## A 100-QUESTION GUIDE TO IMPROVING YOUR RELATIONSHIP

We frequently think we know everything there is to know about our "better half" in a committed relationship, but there is always more to learn! To understand more about your relationship, try asking them each of these 100 questions.
You'll learn things about yourself that you didn't know after answering these 100 questions. Each night during dinner, we suggest taking turns asking and responding to a few questions. Before you know it, you'll be sharing stories from your youth, forecasts for the future, and opinions on hypothetical ideas that you've probably never thought of before.
You are free to omit questions and merely provide a yes or no response, but if you commit to answering each one as completely as possible, you'll increase your chances of success.

Which do you value more: spare time, approval, or money?
Which form of transportation is best or worst? Are you hesitant to fly?
Are you still searching for your life's purpose, or are you already fulfilling it?
What is the finest and worst item you presently have in your fridge?
Are you supportive when others need you?
If you could speak with your 16-year-old self, what would you say?

Tell me three things about me that most people wouldn't know about your love for me.
What was your best job, worst job, and first job ever?
Can you detect when someone is lying or stating the truth?
Do you believe in magic? What time did you encounter it?
What annoys you?
If you had an extra $100 to spend on yourself each week, what would you buy?
Is forgiveness due to everyone?
What's in your pocket or backpack right now?
Do you struggle with any laws or societal conventions?
Have you looked for hints or warnings in your dreams?

Which three items most aid in making you feel prepared for the day?
Do you have any bad habits you'd like to kick?
What is the finest compliment you've ever received?
Do you ever have irrational fears?
Do you think you're currently operating at full capacity?
If you had the option to pick your lenges, would you prefer to keep facing the ones you are currently facing?

Have you ever wanted to be a part of a rock group?
What would your group's name be?
Has a teacher ever had an impact on your life?

Do you ever stick to your resolutions from the previous year?
What household chores do you secretly enjoy carrying out?
What have you ever done that was the most difficult?
When did you last surprise yourself?
Have you ever had a reading from a psychic? Did it turn out to be true?
What mistake do you frequently commit?
Have you ever been forced to apologize in public?
Who has ever come across as the most compassionate to you? What did they do to deserve such kindness?
How many children do you want to have?
Have you ever put more physical pressure than you intended on your body?

For the rest of your life, which movie would you be willing to see each week?
How can you tame your inner judge?
Which of your dreams do you now keep to yourself?
Before checking your phone, how much time do you have?
What was the best piece of advice you ever received?
What adjustments would you make to the economy?
Have you ever fantasized about writing a column that offers suggestions?
What specifically do you want to address first?

Which one, a live-in chef or a live-in massage therapist, would you prefer?
Which of my activities do you wish I would refrain from performing?
What would you do if an unknown donor gave you a large sum of money while requesting that you "Help me solve a problem—any problem!"
Which fragrance do you prefer?
What would you study if you had no time restrictions, the option to enrol in a university course immediately, and your tuition was fully covered by a mysterious benefactor?
If you could meet any literary figure, who would you like to have coffee with?

What would you carry if you were leaving right now on a road trip?
What do you consider to be the ideal age for marriage?
What alterations to your life would social media make if it didn't exist?
What do you regret most?
Do people have a right to happiness?
What would your "pen name" be if you published erotic literature or romance novels?
Is there a problem you're frequently contacted for assistance with?
What do you know? Is it a result of education, personal experience, or both?
What would you like to do if you had time for a new hobby? Would you mind?

What do you have a freakish talent for?

Do you have any physical characteristics that you wish you could change or hide?
What animal best represents you?
Have you ever arranged a date for two friends?
What has been the highlight of your day thus far?
Have you ever had the chance to meet a hero?
What achievement from the previous year gave you the most satisfaction?
Have you ever had real concerns about your physical safety?
What was your worst-ever appearance?

Have you ever stolen something?
Which feat are you most proud of yet have never mentioned on your resume?
If you were utilizing an online dating service to look for dates, what is the key thing that would entice you to a person's profile?
What previous endeavour would you not attempt again?
Have you ever wanted to change your name?

What do you know that is most significant or practical?
Do you prefer to be saved or to save others?
What was the sweetest kiss you've ever received?
Do you believe that anyone can lead?
What decision have you ever made that was the most out of character?
Do you want to pen a screenplay?
What musical instrument, if any, would you learn to play?
What do you consider to be your most appealing quality?
Which of your past dates was the strangest?

What was the lone factor in your romantic life?
Have you received a prize? What did it serve?
Which would you choose: a sociable idiot or a reclusive genius?
What will the name of your upcoming memoir be?
What do you consider the perfect home visitor to be?
Which endangered species would you pick to try to preserve from extinction?
Which of your guilty pleasures is the worst?

What important task is at the top of your list for the rest of the year?
What hymn or song best captures who you are?
Ever come up against a brick wall? How did you get away from there?
What animal did you last see in the wild?
Ever disagreed with a friend and wished you could patch things up?
What do you do when your friends or competitors are buying things you want to buy?
When and where do you come up with the most original ideas?

Do you identify as an ambivert, extrovert, or someone in between?
How do you want your life to be in five years?
Which would you prefer, an additional $300 daily or an additional two hours daily?
How would your ideal home be laid out?
What do you feel most grateful for right now?
How come you thought I was "the one"?

www.ingramcontent.com/pod-product-compliance
Lightning Source LLC
LaVergne TN
LVHW020536160826
845677LV00015B/4087

* 9 7 9 8 3 7 0 3 9 0 6 6 1 *